I Wonder Why

Minibeasts

Karen Wallace and Tudor Humphries

KINGFISHER

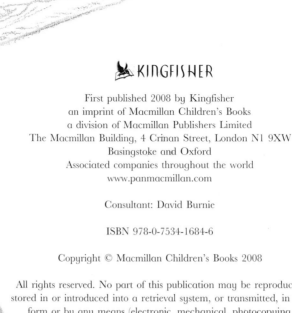

KINGFISHER

First published 2008 by Kingfisher
an imprint of Macmillan Children's Books
a division of Macmillan Publishers Limited
The Macmillan Building, 4 Crinan Street, London N1 9XW
Basingstoke and Oxford
Associated companies throughout the world
www.panmacmillan.com

Consultant: David Burnie

ISBN 978-0-7534-1684-6

Copyright © Macmillan Children's Books 2008

2 4 6 8 9 7 5 3 1

1TR/0408/LFG/UNTD/140MA/C

A CIP record is available from the British Library.

Printed in China

Contents

What are minibeasts?

Minibeasts are tiny animals, such as insects and spiders. They have been on Earth for millions of years and live in all sorts of different places, from hot, wet jungles to cold, rocky mountains.

praying mantis

butterfly

two male stag beetles

4

1. How many legs
   do insects have?

2. How many types of
   insect are there?

3. Are beetles insects?

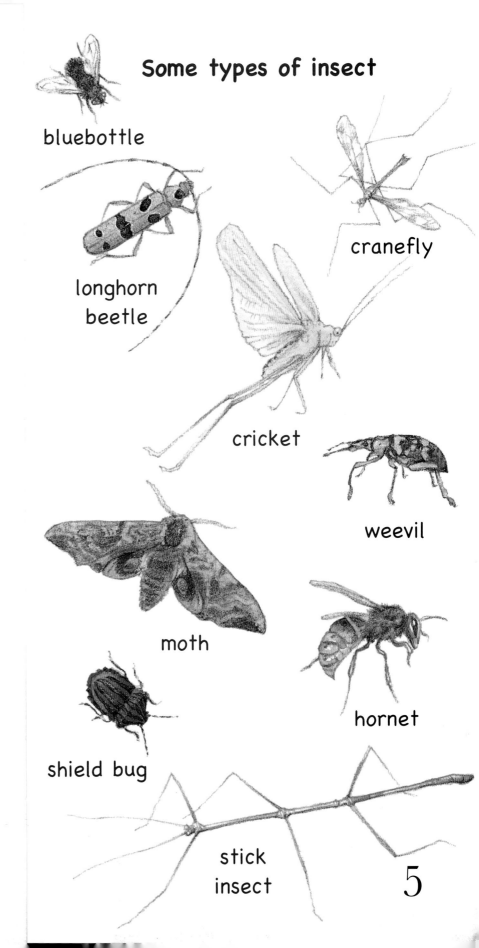

Some types of insect

bluebottle

cranefly

longhorn
beetle

cricket

weevil

moth

hornet

shield bug

stick
insect

5

Ladybirds

Ladybirds are small beetles with wings. They are easy to see because they have colourful, spotted shells. Ladybirds live in gardens and meadows, and have tiny mouths and a pair of jaws.

ladybird on a leaf

ladybirds on flowers

6

1. How do ladybirds smell, taste and feel?

2. Can a ladybird fly?

3. What does a ladybird eat?

ir two
's, to
iste.

otty
ird
protect
ith.

sts
is
s

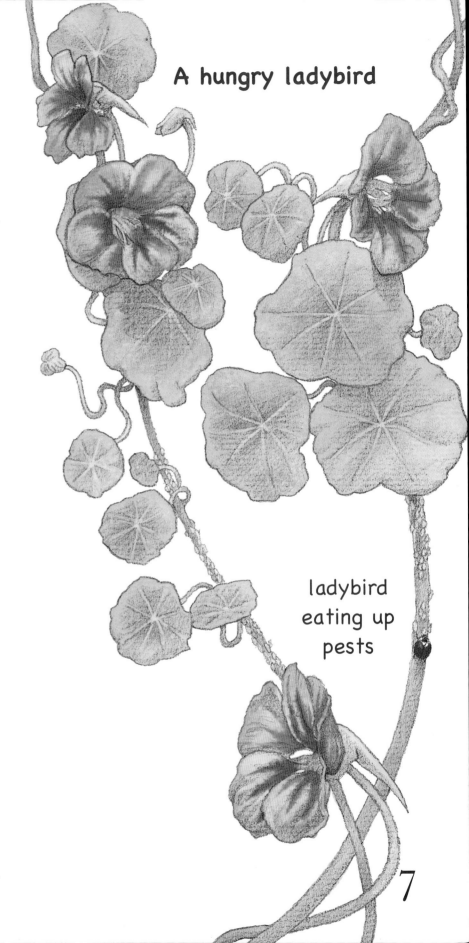

A hungry ladybird

ladybird
eating up
pests

Ants

Ants are busy insects that live in large groups. Some make their nests under stones, in the ground, or inside logs or trees. Wood ants make their nests inside a giant pile of dead leaves.

queen ant flying

wood ants' nest

1. Can any ants fly?

2. How many ants live in a nest?

3. Why do some ants cut up leaves?

se

l.

jaws.

e

od.

Butterflies

There are many types of butterfly. Some of them fly a long way to spend winter in warm sunshine. Most butterflies feed on flowers. They suck up their food through a long, hollow mouth.

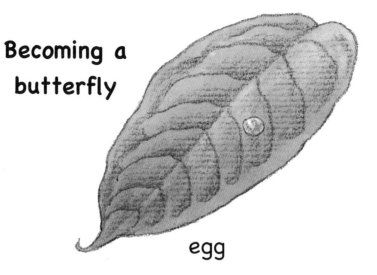

egg

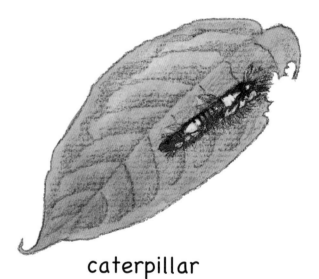

caterpillar

butterfly on a flower

mouth curled up

10

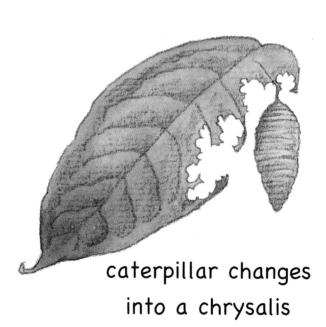

caterpillar changes into a chrysalis

1. How many eggs do butterflies lay?

2. How does a caterpillar turn into a butterfly?

3. Which butterfly has extra-strong wings?

Monarch butterflies flying south in the winter

Spiders

There are over 40,000 different types of spider. They can be smaller than a tip of a pencil or bigger than a dinner plate. All spiders can grow a new leg if one breaks.

Mexican redknee tarantula

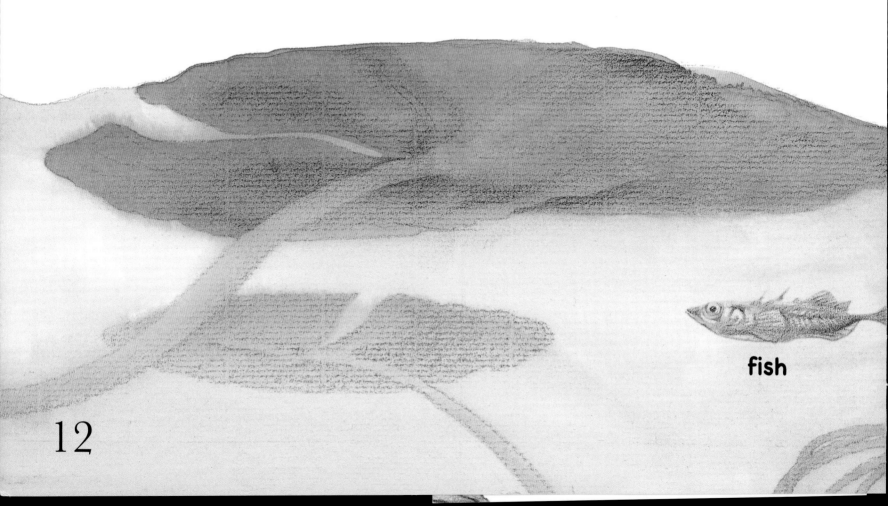

fish

1. No. Many spiders, such as this Mexican redknee tarantula, live in burrows underground.

2. A spider makes silk inside its body. To build a web, it squirts out the silk in a long line and sticks it in place.

3. A water spider's long, hairy legs help the spider catch its food.

Building a web

building lines of silk

the web is finished

Honeybees

Honeybees make their nests from wax. Inside the nest, there are thousands of small spaces, called cells. Some cells are used to store honey, and the queen bee lays her eggs in others.

honeybee nest

honeybees flying

14

1. Honeybees do a special dance to tell other bees in the nest where the best flowers are growing.

2. Honeybees suck nectar, a sugary water, from flowers. They turn this into honey inside their bodies.

3. In spring, a queen bee can lay over two thousand eggs a day.

In the nest

queen honeybee laying eggs

worker honeybee feeding a grub (baby bee)

young honeybee climbing out of a cell

15

Dragonflies

Dragonflies live by ponds and lakes. They are speedy hunters that feed on smaller insects. Some hover in the air and chase after their food. Others lie in wait, snatching up insects that come too close.

dragonfly

Once, dragonflies were huge.

16

1. Do dragonflies
have eyes?

2. Why do dragonflies
have four wings?

3. How long have
dragonflies lived
on Earth?

eye

dragonfly

Dragonflies are
smaller today.

1. Dragonflies have the largest eyes of all insects.

2. Dragonflies can move their wings in different directions. They can fly forwards or backwards to escape danger.

3. Dragonflies have lived on Earth for 300 million years. They were around even before the dinosaurs!

A dragonfly in danger

hungry toad lying in wait

dragonfly flying backwards

Index